MW01437908

dark acre

dark acre

poems by

Canese Jarboe

Acme Poem Company
Willow Springs Books
Spokane, Washington

ACKNOWLEDGEMENTS

To Robert Wrigley, with my deepest gratitude.

To the editors and staff of the following publications in which these poems have previously appeared, some in earlier versions: *Hayden's Ferry Review*, *Indiana Review*, *TYPO*, *Muzzle*, *Noble/Gas Quarterly*, *Queen Mob's Teahouse*, *Puerto del Sol*, and *Willow Springs*.

To friends and teachers who have supported me and offered their invaluable insight: Kim Barnes, Michael McGriff, Alexandra Teague, Laura Lee Washburn, Shamala Gallagher, Jason Mastaler, Tara Howe, Wendy Silva, Zana Previti, Michael Landreth, Corey Oglesby, Garrett Chavis, Cameron McGill, Stacy Boe Miller, Samantha Burns, Ash Goedker, Lauren Westerfield, Jess McDermott, Sarah VanGundy, Naomi Shihab Nye, Allison Joseph, and Mary Szybist. A special thank-you to my Willow Springs Books editor, Cass Bruner, and the staff.

To The Frost Place, especially Maudelle Driskell, Dawn Potter, and Kerrin McCadden.

To my beloved family.

To Nat Fisher, my partner-in-poetry. All my love and wild gratitude.

dark acre is Volume 8 in the Acme Poem Company Surrealist Poetry Series.

No part of this book may be reproduced or transmitted in any form or by any means, electronic or mechanical, including photography, recording, or any information storage or retrieval system now known or to be invented, without permission from the publisher, except by a reviewer who wishes to quote brief passages in connection with a review written for inclusion in a magazine, newspaper, or broadcast.

Cataloging and Publication Information available from the Library of Congress on request.

Cover Art: *Untitled* by Pat Perry. This and other works can be found at http://patperry.net/
Cover Design: Taylor Waring
Interior Layout: Cassandra Bruner

FIRST EDITION

Willow Springs Books, Spokane, WA 99202
Copyright © 2018 Canese Jarboe
Printed in the United States of America
All Rights Reserved
Printed by Gray Dog Press
ISBN: 978-0-9990050-1-9

This and other Willow Springs Books titles may be viewed online at willowspringsbooks.org.

TABLE OF CONTENTS

Using a Stolen Guide on Morse Code, I Send a Signal
    out My Bedroom Window into the Cornfield — 11

Landscape w/ My Father & a Dead Man's Harmonica — 12

Girlhood (7) — 14

Rodeo Queen — 15

Erica Jong Said, "If a Woman Wants to Be a Poet,
    She Must Dwell in the House of the Tomato," — 16

Girlhood (2) — 18

Rapunzel w/ a Ruby Red Grapefruit — 19

Girlhood (4) — 20

Brother, I Built This Diorama
    of My Nightmare inside a Shoebox for You — 21

Girlhood w/ Rattlesnake — 22

Girlhood (6) — 23

Herbal Abortion — 24

Triptych w/ Stunt Cock — 25

Rapunzel w/ Head Half-Shaved — 26

Dark Acre — 27

"And then we are closer and closer to being our own gravediggers"

-Guillaume Apollinaire, "Océan de Terre" (as trans. by Roger Shattuck)

USING A STOLEN GUIDE ON MORSE CODE, I SEND A SIGNAL OUT MY BEDROOM WINDOW INTO THE CORNFIELD

••

•− −−

••• − •• •−•• •−••

•••• • •−• •

•−•−•−

LANDSCAPE W/ MY FATHER & A DEAD MAN'S HARMONICA

The Missouri state line is as good a place as any to kill yourself.
After he bought the farm,

                                        he thought you static on the TV.

He thought you dripping dark honey
onto the ceiling fan for months, too hot for the hive in the attic to hold.

When he heard the harmonica past midnight,

                            it was you.

———

In the sink
       —the china with the mutable pattern of black ants.

———

Minerals. To strengthen asphalt shingles, granules

                                          of oyster shells & mica.

I think they use zinc now, to keep algae from growing

              —to keep the roof   a reflective black ocean.
This is where my father lives:
                        always nail gun,
always steel-toe,
always linoleum knife.   He forgot the tarp & me,

                              a midnight bride with a 40-foot train.

       There was someone in the rafters that night, watching
a girl disappear into a   darker field.

                              I still wonder who is waiting
               in the rafters—who,   in their nest

         of flannel work shirts, will steal the tractor?
                              ———

He made a face for me: cow pelvis fixed
to the inside of a welding helmet.

                              ———

        gunoilgunoilgunoilgunoilgunoilgunoilgunoilgunoilgunoil

       My father has a harmonica &
                       he is playing a song I don't know.

GIRLHOOD (7)

i paint

my nipples gold &

since my first

communion

i've practiced

being a figurine

so

everyone

would kiss

my soft metal

unrecognizable

RODEO QUEEN

Inside my skull, I keep a miniature saddle
made of bone.
     We all have a miniature saddle
inside. It isn't rider-less   yet. O pituitary gland,
       I want to be alone now.
I remember a horse in a parade with glittery, pink hooves.
I remember when I had glittery, pink hooves &
  stood underneath the grandstand / waiting
    to give a blowjob at the county fair.
Even with a cock in your mouth, watching a barrel racer
  between a thousand boots
        feels private, somehow.
    Still.
   There has always been a saddle,
but never a horse (& this has never upset me
    because I could just rub myself silly
against the leather).
   When I'm alone,   sometimes I wonder
    if I could even hold on.

ERICA JONG SAID, "IF A WOMAN WANTS TO BE A POET, SHE MUST DWELL IN THE HOUSE OF THE TOMATO,"

1

& a tomato is a tomato is a tomato is my pussy
    —I forget they are fruit.

    2

    Wolf peach. The scientific
    name for tomato means *wolf*
    peach, *lycopersicum*, after a rumor
    that witches used deadly
    nightshade to turn themselves into
    werewolves (when what a witch
        really does is:

            apply flying ointment
            & masturbate with her broomstick).

3

I canned hot salsa until I entombed myself in row upon row

                of superheated glass.

4

o flavr savr   o ripening   o goodbye

    5

    This is the fuzz of me, the soft, dark
        worm of me. I am mining this
        fruit & tunneling
        this Tunnel of My Exact Dimensions,
        until

        silver moth
        silver moth
        silver moth

& not long for this.

GIRLHOOD (2)

we rub ourselves wildly

at the foot of your chair

—you can't see us all

the way down here

RAPUNZEL W/ A RUBY RED GRAPEFRUIT

Mostly, the intimacy of red is too much
for morning. My tongue, I hold with sugar

spoon. I could eat a whole magnolia
blossom, full-bloom/silver filling

in his back tooth/two blonde French
braids/red clay and bull thistle, a ditch full.

Why is this the inside of everything? It is
catfish heart or pussy or tomato rotting

or peony or you. I don't keep my sweet
where you think. I keep it in my spit. I tell

the waitress *I don't need no honey*/drool
unbroken over all this blush.

GIRLHOOD (4)

inside, our father

wishes we

were born calves

BROTHER, I BUILT THIS DIORAMA
OF MY NIGHTMARE INSIDE A SHOEBOX FOR YOU

I needed a moon,

but there wasn't one. I poked too many stars

with a sewing needle. There are 70 acres

of coconut flakes with green food coloring,

but I don't know if we ever make it to the edges.

We can't see

our mother with a paring knife

looking for the bad spot.

At first, I think we are the pond

made of aluminum foil, but I am

you with a clean face. I am you without

your favorite heels and I am running.

Somewhere,

a man yells *faggot* in red puff paint.

Here is the gap in the fence

made for your body.

GIRLHOOD W/ RATTLESNAKE

who taught you

to control

your venom

or

did you

teach yourself

GIRLHOOD (6)

i tape my maxi-pad
to the ceiling to stop it leaking

HERBAL ABORTION

when I say *I lived in a cave that summer*, what
I really mean is aluminum camper full of salamanders. no,
I mean I lived inside my own womb

dripping stalactites, soda straws salt-bright. inside
the warm mini-fridge: a lake.   bottomless.   [one
I saw when I went spelunking

with the science club in berryville, arkansas].
what if there was a headlamp
for that kind of darkness?

when I say *I was a black bear*, I mean
the way they mate.   together & alone.   he sniffed
my urine, chewed on my neck.   disappeared.

when I say *I foraged*, what I mean
is midnight parsley tea, mega-dose of vitamin c,
waited until dark to find acre of miniature
stars/pulled up evening primrose   & devoured
root system, blossom.

TRIPTYCH W/ STUNT COCK

Lord, have mercy. I am full of minnows
rubbing their disco-ball bellies over
all my penetralia. Part-time bimbo
—nylon thong I bedazzled with river
rocks. Could you get this bee out of my hair?

Could you just get this bee out of my hair?
Camera Man psyched about the rented pool.
Neosporin Pussy Queen & all bare,
my braid doubles as a leash if you pull
hard enough. This ball gag making me drool.

Harder. This ball gag is making me drool.
Remember the bait shop? Styrofoam. Night-
crawlers. I am a go-cup of alive
& I think that if you held me real tight
you would feel everything unknot. You might.

RAPUNZEL W/ HEAD HALF-SHAVED

    This peony too heavy to hold itself
up. This great blue heron in slow-mo, opportunistic
feeder. This rash. This calamine lotion. Be vibrating
my skull. I am looking for sick fish. No,
algal bloom. There wasn't any juice in the fridge
so I drank the cattle vaccine. Let me
come back as an orange flag marking a utility line or
a rain gauge. Let me come back as aluminum, tetanus,
and Sure-Jell. I am listening for the last seal
to pop. Vacuum. Long-legged or nesting 100' above you.
This fiberglass insulation like pink
cotton-candy. This angle. This respirator. I don't think you can hear me
over the air compressor. *At 10:04 p.m. National Weather Service
Doppler Radar indicated a severe*

capable of

                                         an   interior room

               use blankets   or pillows

     your body
, in the nearest ditch.

DARK ACRE

If you asked me to witch

for water I could If you asked me

to witch for a sewer line I could I'll be

the first to tell you I can't find

a damn thing up here No such thing

as a dowsing rod for alive

A thing inside of a thing inside of a thing: on the cover of the book a boy and a girl read a book: on the cover of that book, the boy and the girl read a book: and on the cover of that book, the boy and the girl read a book until all our yellow roses vanish:
Every owl has a gizzard: and every gizzard is a witch bottle inside of an owl: Claws: Skulls: Feathers: all perfectly capable of deflecting a hex:

Born with all the eggs I will ever have: Ovarian: one million: two million:

These locusts been waiting seventeen years to see me in my nightgown.

Are you above or below?

I am an apex predator. You are an apex predator.
We have an inter-predator relationship.

Some species of owl do not have a shadow.
They break moonlight over their bodies—an owl is an optical illusion.
They are either the color of air or the color of dirt,
depending on your orientation.

Are you above or below?

I have been Queen for ten minutes in the glass cab of a tractor, the control
panel blossoming & blossoming. I don't remember this
because of the murder-suicide, I remember the murder-suicide because of this

& also this:

the mural of lightning & calculating

   the math of safety:

      one-mississippi
      two-mississippi

Away from lightning rods The positive charges rise
through our hair The higher the hair the closer to Jesus

Center-stage, there is a block &
tackle (hanging
from a barn rafter)
reserved for butchering deer,
but I am a showgirl
riding the pulley down from the hayloft
—a thousand tiny spotlights trained on me
through holes in the roof

    There is a gateway to hell in the woods behind my house.

                I am standing

  in a room

                      full of taxidermy

      ducks

                  suspended

                          in flight.

I am the daughter of the seer of Crawford County.
He keeps his Catalogue of Death beside the bed.
I don't look inside.

            openthedooropenthedooropenthedooropenthedooropenthedoor

sometimes I am my daddy and I chomp on the barrel of a gun

Dear [   ],

Why did you stop walking for an entire year?

[   ] could only crawl backward on all fours:
        lame calf my father might have shot, until
every cabinet, every appliance was an obstacle, indistinguishable
        landscape, until [   ] was lost
inside the house [   ] was raised in.

There is an owl outside my window again.

We have a conversation from my bed.

The only deaths he predicts
are the ones that never happen/are the ones
that always happen

        After all,

somebody surely died on a gravel road tonight
       surely

Do you think I am under a curse?

A banshee is just a rumor that a barn owl started.

I still believe she will come for you
with neon fish stringer,
floating: metal pin through your heart
& your death erection.

        My fingers are fillet knives:

                                          they've got to be.

If you look inside the refrigerator If you look
inside the styrofoam cup There
is a very still luna moth that will fly
if we take her out on this warm night This
is how you survive

ACME POEM COMPANY

Willow Springs Books is a small literary press housed in Eastern Washington University's MFA program in Spokane, Washington. Its annual chapbook series selects and publishes contemporary surrealist poetry under the auspices of the Acme Poem Company.

PREVIOUS COLLECTIONS

Black Postcards, Michael McGriff
The 9-Day Queen Gets Lost on Her Way to the Execution, Karyna McGlynn
Startle Pattern, Larissa Szporluk
Drunk on Salt, James Nolan
You Won't Need That, Robert Gregory
Gnawing on a Thin Man, Ray Amorosi
No Time for Dancing, Adam Hammer

For a complete list of selections from Willow Springs Books and ordering information, visit www.willowspringsbooks.org.

Willow Springs Books staff who contributed to this chapbook were Cassandra Bruner, Tessa Bryant, Austin Fuller, Lauren Hohle, Kim Kent, Maura Lammers, Tania Nuñez-Guzman, Nathaniel Sand, Leona Vander Molen, and Taylor Waring.